The Middle School Manual

To all of the students that I know and to the ones I have never met...

You've Got This!

The Middle School Manual

Table of Contents

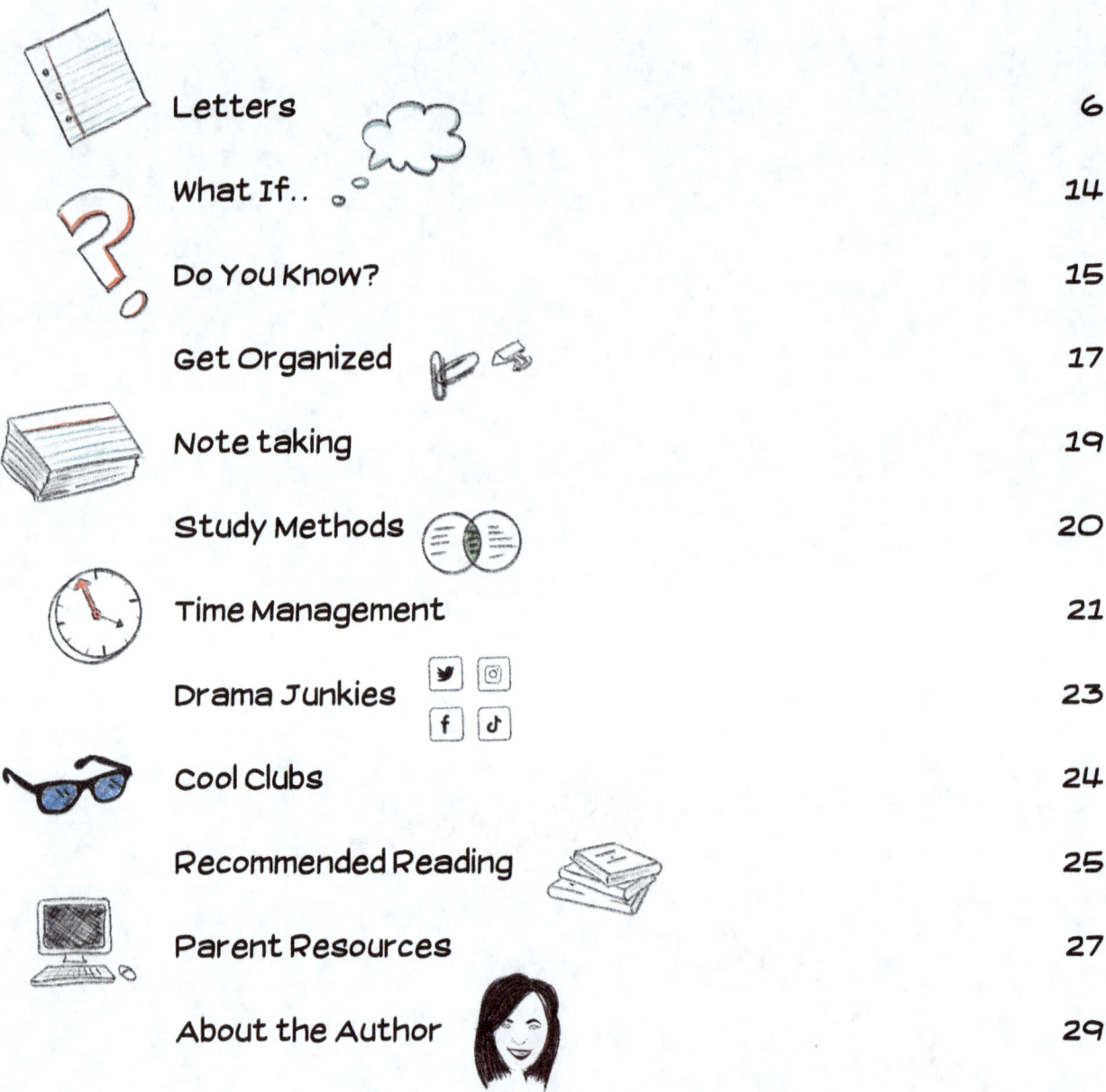

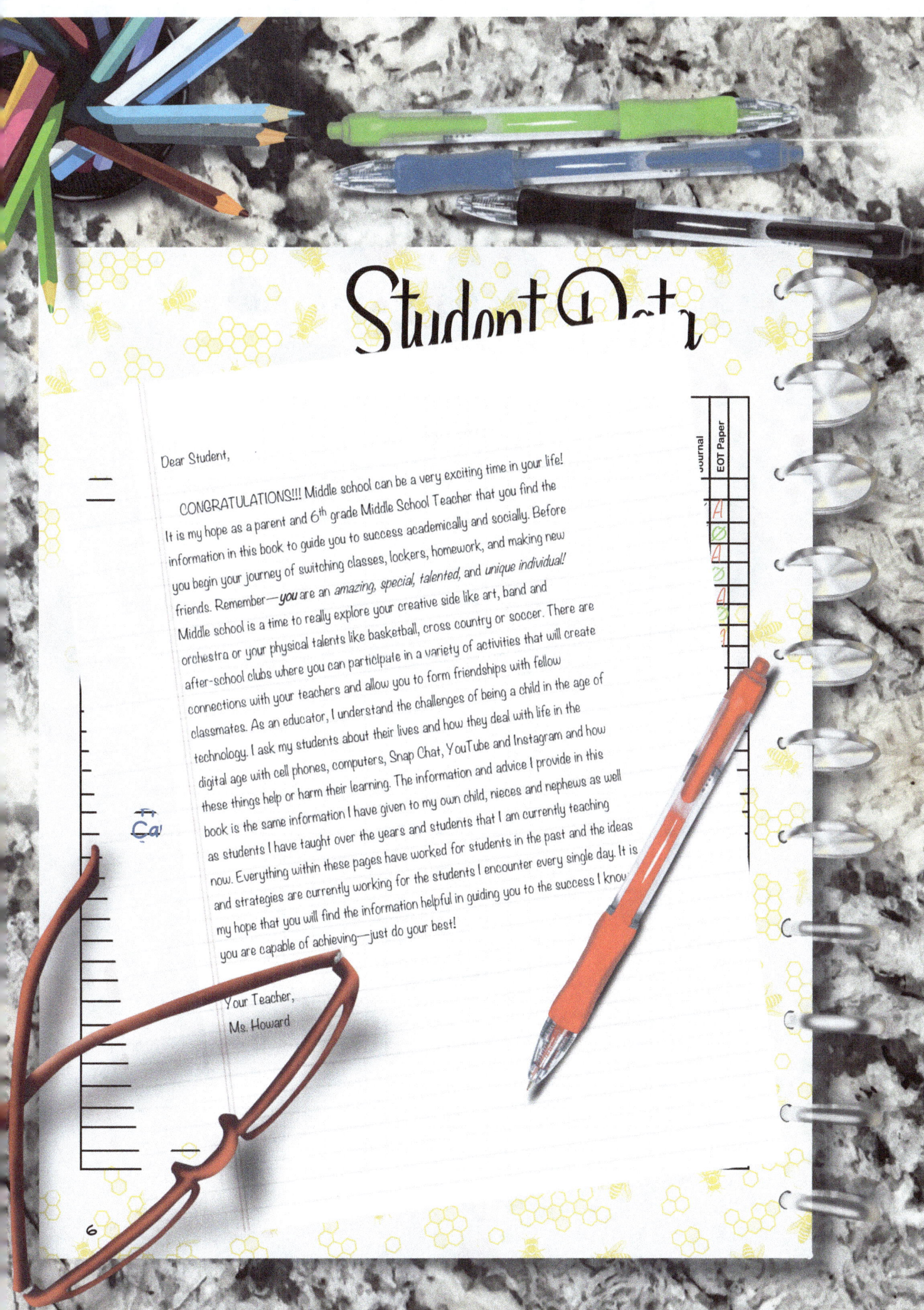

Dear Student,

CONGRATULATIONS!!! Middle school can be a very exciting time in your life! It is my hope as a parent and 6th grade Middle School Teacher that you find the information in this book to guide you to success academically and socially. Before you begin your journey of switching classes, lockers, homework, and making new friends. Remember—**you** are an *amazing, special, talented,* and *unique individual!* Middle school is a time to really explore your creative side like art, band and orchestra or your physical talents like basketball, cross country or soccer. There are after-school clubs where you can participate in a variety of activities that will create connections with your teachers and allow you to form friendships with fellow classmates. As an educator, I understand the challenges of being a child in the age of technology. I ask my students about their lives and how they deal with life in the digital age with cell phones, computers, Snap Chat, YouTube and Instagram and how these things help or harm their learning. The information and advice I provide in this book is the same information I have given to my own child, nieces and nephews as well as students I have taught over the years and students that I am currently teaching now. Everything within these pages have worked for students in the past and the ideas and strategies are currently working for the students I encounter every single day. It is my hope that you will find the information helpful in guiding you to the success I know you are capable of achieving—just do your best!

Your Teacher,
Ms. Howard

WEEK of _____

MONTH
AUGUST
MONTH

MONDAY

Tips from Super Savy 6th Graders!

TUESDAY

WEDNESDAY

THURSDAY

FRIDAY

SATURDAY

SUNDAY

NOTES

Dear Future 6th Grader,

I know you are saying to yourself, "Wow, I'm growing up." If you think you're going to be "Grown up," REALITY CHECK! That's not how it works. If you come to school with a good attitude, you will be fine. At my school if you have good behavior, you will have many privileges. I know that you are all worried about your locker — 2 words, don't worry for about the first 2 weeks, it'll take you some time which is normal. Just remember, don't share your combination with anyone. You have to get to class on time — this is where responsibility and commitment come in. The good thing is, you have a warning bell that lets you know you have 1 minute to get to class.

Be safe. Be responsible. Be respectful.

Sincerely,

Jillian

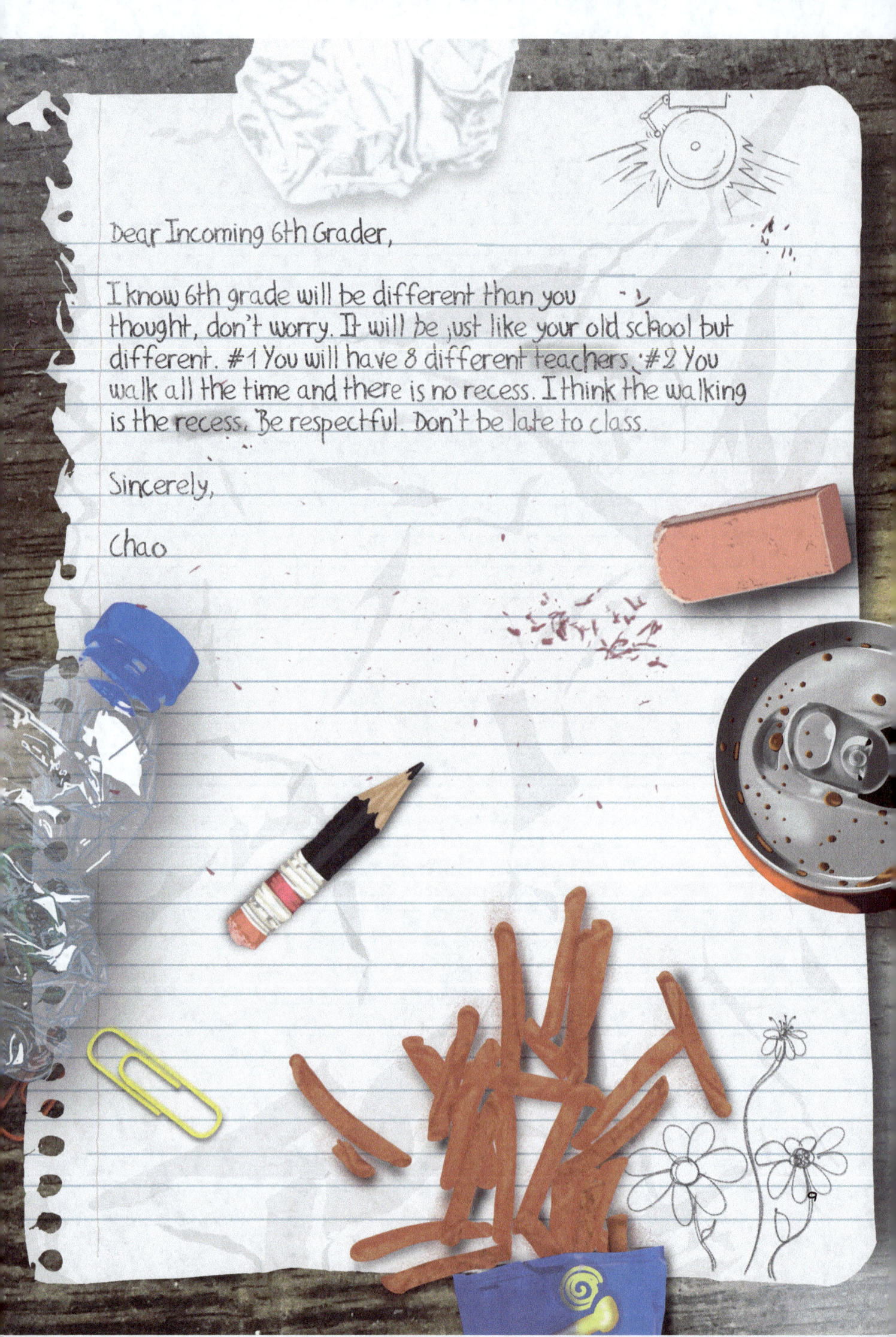

Dear Incoming 6th Grader,

I know 6th grade will be different than you thought, don't worry. It will be just like your old school but different. #1 You will have 8 different teachers. #2 You walk all the time and there is no recess. I think the walking is the recess. Be respectful. Don't be late to class.

Sincerely,

Chao

Dear 5th Grader

Do you think you know everything about middle school? You carry your binder everywhere you go. In fact, your binder is the most important thing other than homework. Your locker is important too! Tip: NEVER, EVER, share a locker with anybody. The person you share your locker with can easily steal your belongings. Homework is easy, just take your time. If you do it the day it's assigned, you won't have to worry. Use these tips wisely.

Good Luck!
Mariat

10

Dear Soon to be Middle Schooler,

Hi. I am Hailey. Today, I am writing you for some tips for middle school. You go from being in 1 class to going to 8 different classes. There is going to be homework of course, more kids, more teachers, lockers and grades. Take it from me, do the homework the day it is assigned because it helps your thinking and memory. It also helps you to develop positive study skills and habits that will serve you well throughout life. Sometimes you have study halls where you can get some of your homework done. Now, for grades, grades are really important. Good grades boost your confidence. Grades are really important. Lockers are pretty easy to get the hang of. When I tried to open my locker for the first time, it was a little confusing, but there will be people there to help you. All of the teachers are really nice, and you can ask them any questions. They respect you and what you have to say, so you should show respect to them as well, and read over your notes!

Sincerely,

Hailey R.

Dear Future 6th Grader,

I am writing to you about what to expect in middle school. First, you will have to follow the pattern of a different schedule. Another tip is to keep your things organized and clean. If you don't, then you will loose things that you will need in the future. One last piece of advice is if you need help, teachers are always willing to lend a helping hand.

Sincerely,

Suzanne

Dear Future Sixth Grader,

I was very nervous going into junior high, but you don't have to be! Here are some tips on sixth grade and what to expect. First of all, lockers! Lockers aren't even that hard and with a couple of tries it becomes easy. Homework. The homework is pretty simple, but you have to do it the day you get it, so you don't forget, and: The knowledge is still fresh in your mind. Never ever be late to a class. The tardiness add up and you can get detention. Try and not miss school because you miss out on so much in just one day. I hope you feel less nervous and mentally ready for junior High!

Good Luck,

Lawrence

what if...

I don't understand what the teacher is teaching? Raise your hand and ask your teacher to explain it again or give an example.

I'm afraid to ask questions in class? Immediately after class, ask your teacher for a time that you can get one on one help.

I am absent? If your teacher doesn't have an absent folder, remind him/her you were out.

I'm being picked on? Immediately tell a teacher, counselor or principal.

I'm having trouble at home? Speak with a teacher you connect with or ask to see your counselor.

I think a class is boring or uninteresting? Ask yourself, "What can I learn from this class?" "Why is it important to know a noun from a proper noun?"

I am having trouble with my identity? Speak to a teacher you trust or your counselor.

I am sad or lonely and don't know why? Your counselor or teacher you connect with can help.

14

Do You Know?

Adequate **sleep** is key to doing well in school! You want to be alert and ready to learn but it will be difficult to do if you are sleepy! Middle School Students need at least 8 hours of sleep each night!   **www.kidshealth.org**

If you are **texting** on your phone or going through your favorite apps right before bedtime, you will not get deep sleep. Deep sleep is very important for your brain, memory and overall health. **www.sleepfoundation.org**

If you are **hungry,** you cannot solve problems, memorize information or focus. Whether it's a granola bar or yogurt, students need something in their tummy to turn on their brain! **www.healthychildren.org**

Drinking **water** is crucial for overall health! Most schools allow students to carry a reusable water bottle. Staying hydrated will improve your mood and memory! **https://www.cdc.gov/ healthy-weight-growth/water-healthy-drinks/index.html**

If you **exercise** now, you will age well! Exercise improves your mental and physical health. **https://www.mayoclinichealthsystem.org/hometown-health/speaking-of-health/ teens-and-exercise**

Do You Know?

It is best to **study** every night so you can ace your tests! Studies have shown that students who attempt to cram the night before an exam do not perform as well as students who study every night over the course of a week or two. **https://www.thetutorteam.com/study-skills/5-reasons-why-good-study-skills-are-important/**

If you **journal**, you will improve your overall mental health. Writing down your thoughts and feelings is a good way to reflect and release. **https://youtu.be/TE9Vp7jpho8?si=HGnJI2hO3-oyzR5b**

If your **room** is a mess, your mind is a mess! CLEAN YOUR ROOM! It will make you feel accomplished and it shows off your organizational skills. **https://raisingteenstoday.com/hey-teens-heres-the-real-reason-you-should-clean-your-bedroom/**

School Counselors are there to **help** you succeed academically, emotionally and socially! **www.educationadvanced.com**

Reading is a great way to exercise your brain! **www.youngreadersfoundation.org** Please go to the link and click on The Importance of Reading and read the 15 reasons why you should read everyday!

Get Organized

Step1: Take your Sharpie and label your composition or spiral notebooks for your core classes: English, Math, Science, Social Studies

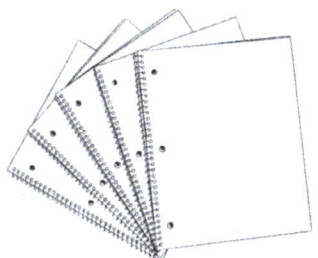  

Step 2: Label the outside of your folders for your core classes: English, Math, Science, Social Studies.

Step 3: Label the inside of your folders.

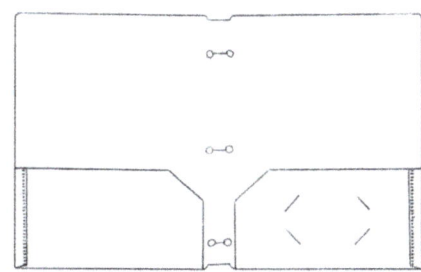

Step 4: Label your pocket tab dividers.

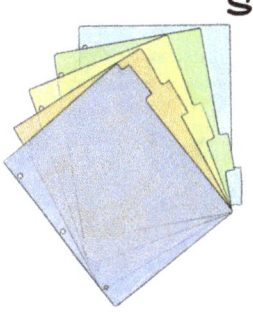

step 5: Put your labeled tab dividers with your labeled composition or spiral notebooks in your 3 ring binder.

Notetaking

✖ Start at the beginning of your notebook. Always make sure you use the correct notebook for the appropriate class.

✖ Fold the right corner of the paper and write the date.

✖ **whatever the teacher writes on the board, you write in your notebook!**

✖ Underline important words.

✖ Put a question mark (?) next to any words or concepts that you need the teacher to review, explain or provide a detailed example.

✖ Use the loose-leaf paper if you forget your binder or run out of room in your notebook.

✖ Remember, after school all notes must be put in the same place, so you may need to rewrite them and put them in the notebook.

Cornell Notes are designed to keep your notes organized so you can review and refresh yourself with information. Although Cornell notetaking comes in various forms, I decided to keep it simple with **Key Points, Details and Summary.**

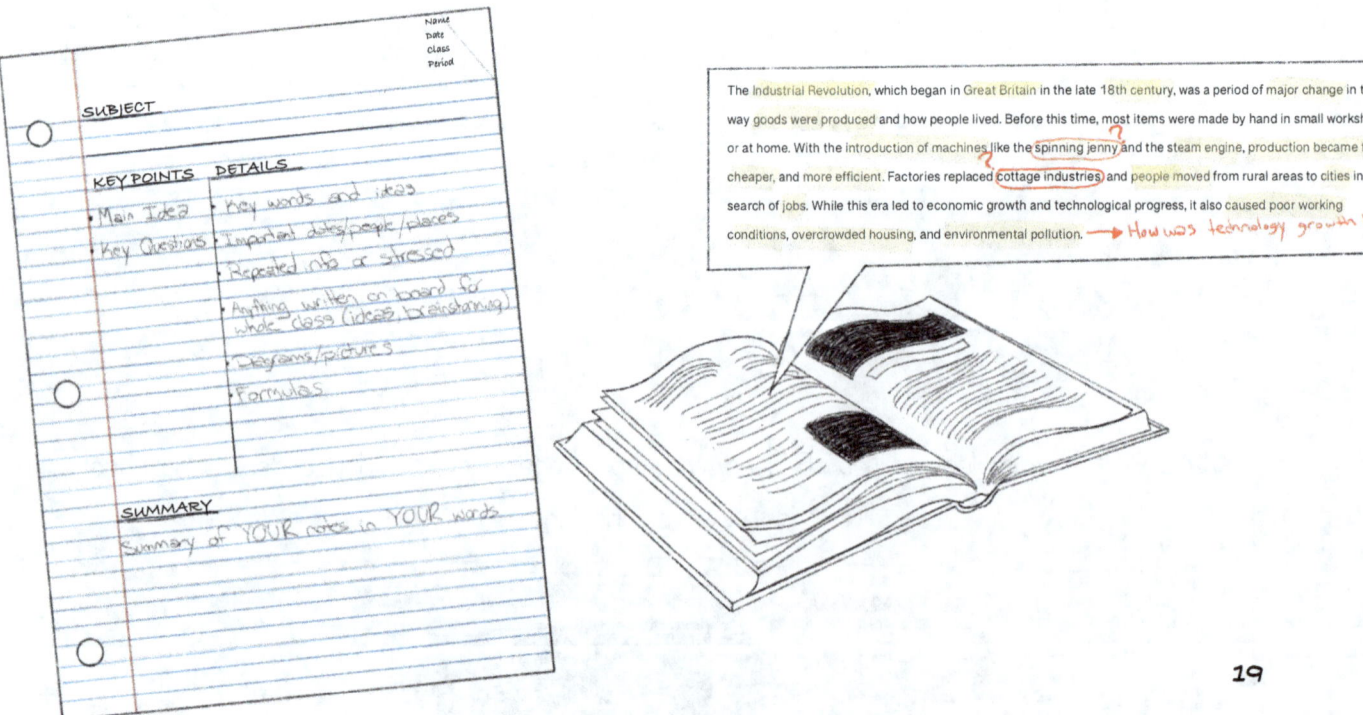

Study Methods

SQ3R
(Study, Question, Read, Recite, Review)

1. Take an index card
2. Write your initials on the top right corner
3. Write the word, question, equation, etc. on the front
4. Write definition or the answer on the back
5. Keep your cards in a zip lock bag or with a rubber band around them.

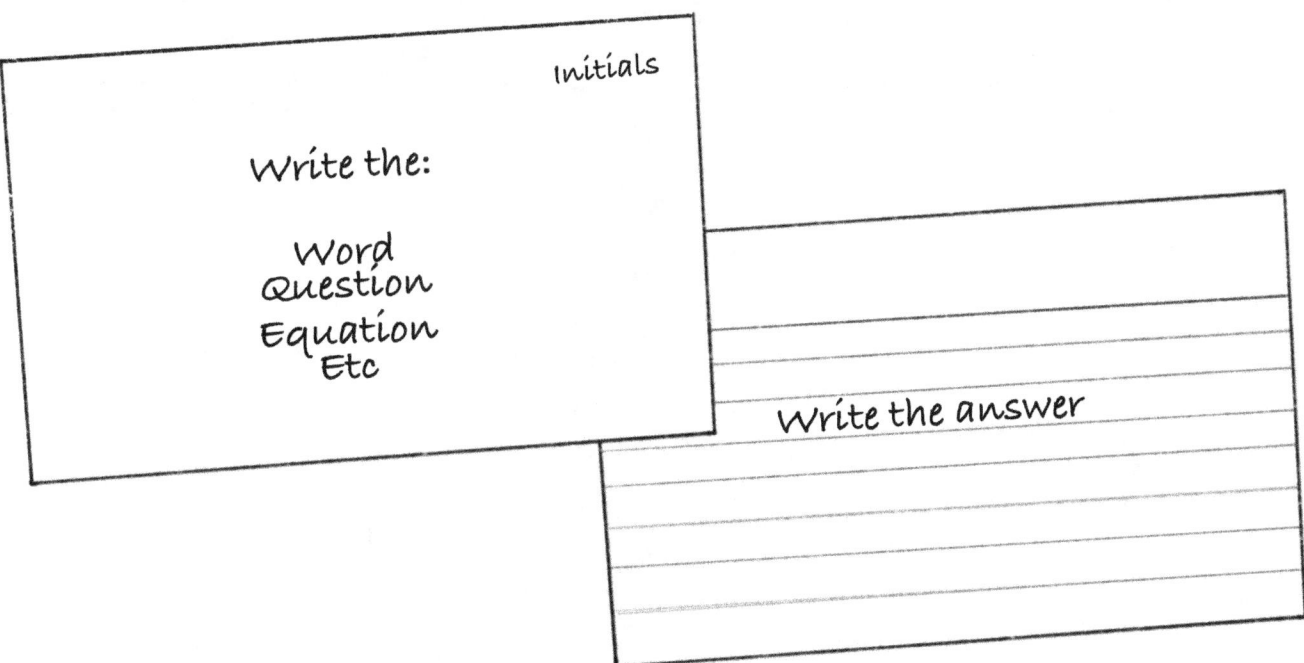

Another great way to study is to reread/review your notes, recite important information **ALOUD!** I know it sounds silly but most students learn by the reading the material, speaking the material and by seeing the material.

Time Management

"If you fail to plan, you are planning to fail."
Benjamin Franklin

Managing your time is a major factor in your success. Whether you have extra-curricular activities or not, time management is just as important as being organized. Never put off your homework. Always start with your hardest subject first —avoiding it will not help you learn. Your teacher will appreciate the effort your put in and it will help you later in life to tackle challenges. You will feel better about yourself and on the path to academic success if you use your time wisely.

Write your assignments in your school agenda, planner or calendar that fits your binder.

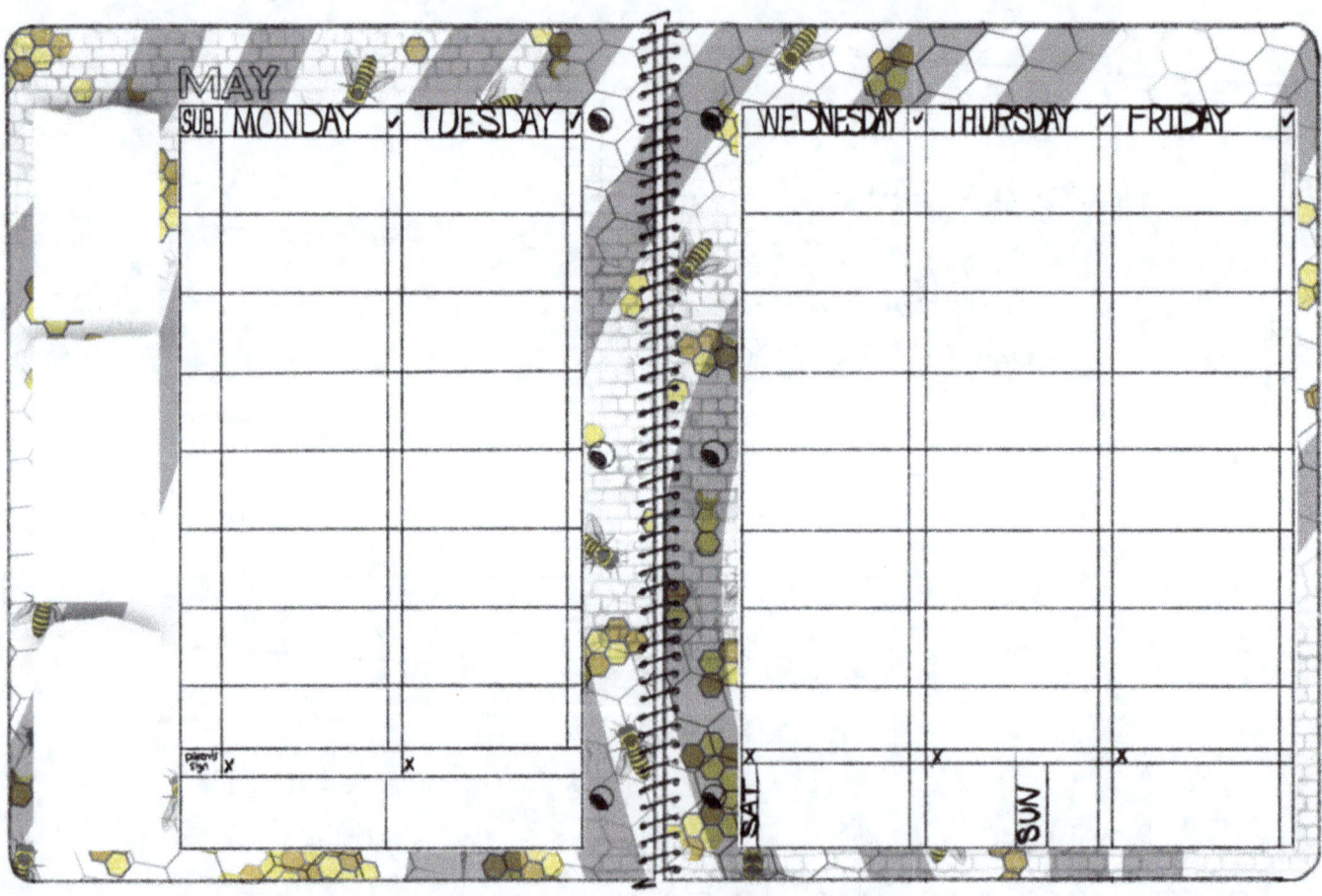

There are time management apps that you can download into your phone: Google calender, in Class, myhomework, Mytimeorganizer and TempoSmartCalendar.

In addition to an agenda or a traditional calender, you can create a simple time block.

This is an example of a time block schedule for a student with homework and soccer practice.

Periods	Time	Mon	Tues	Wed	Thu	Fri
1	8:00-9:26	A	A	B	A	C
2	9:33-11:00	B	C	C	B	D
	11:05-11:30	Lunch A				
	11:30-11:55	Lunch B				
3	12:00-1:26	D	F	D	F	F
4	1:33-3:00	E	G	E	G	E
After	3:30-5:30	Practice	Practice	HW	Practice	HW
School	5:30-7:30	Dinner	Dinner	Scrimage	Dinner	Dinner
	7:30-9:30	HW	HW	Dinner	HW	Game

Tips:

 Turn OFF your cellphone or put your phone on "Do Not Disturb," during homework/study time.

 Complete each and every assignment one by one until it is completely finished.

 Do not play video games on school nights.

 Do not stay up late! Middle Schoolers need at least 8 hours of sleep!

Drama Junkies aka DJ's

Q: What is a **"Drama Junkie?"**

A: A person who cannot function without being the cause, instigator or participant of a problem or ongoing problems.

DJ's can be seen doing one or a combination of unsavory behaviors:
- Bullying
- Disrupts the class—all of the time!
- Disrespects classmates and the teacher(s)
- Fights/picks fights
- Keeps drama going with "he said," "she said" gossip
- Refuses to comply with classroom and/or school rules

Advice: 1. <u>Never</u> befriend one! 2. <u>Do not become one!</u>

If you have the unfortunate task of being paired in class with a DJ or if a DJ tries to befriend you **<u>remain calm, do not engage in lengthy conversation, do not make eye contact and ignore their disruptive behavor. Do not spend time in or out of of school with a DJ!</u>**

Drama Junkies are looking for attention—do not allow them to pull you into their chaos! Anytime you feel anxious, overwhelmed or stressed, go see your school counselor or speak to a teacher you have a connection with.

Cool Clubs

Check out the clubs that are avaliable at your school. The list is to give you an idea of some of the clubs that are offered—remember all schools are different!

African American Scholars

Athletics (basketball, cross-country, soccer, tennis, track and field, etc.)

Book Club

Cooking Club

Educators Rising (Formerly FEA)

Garden Club

Girls Club

Intramural Sports

Math Club

Robotics Club

Science Club

Spelling/Spell Bowl

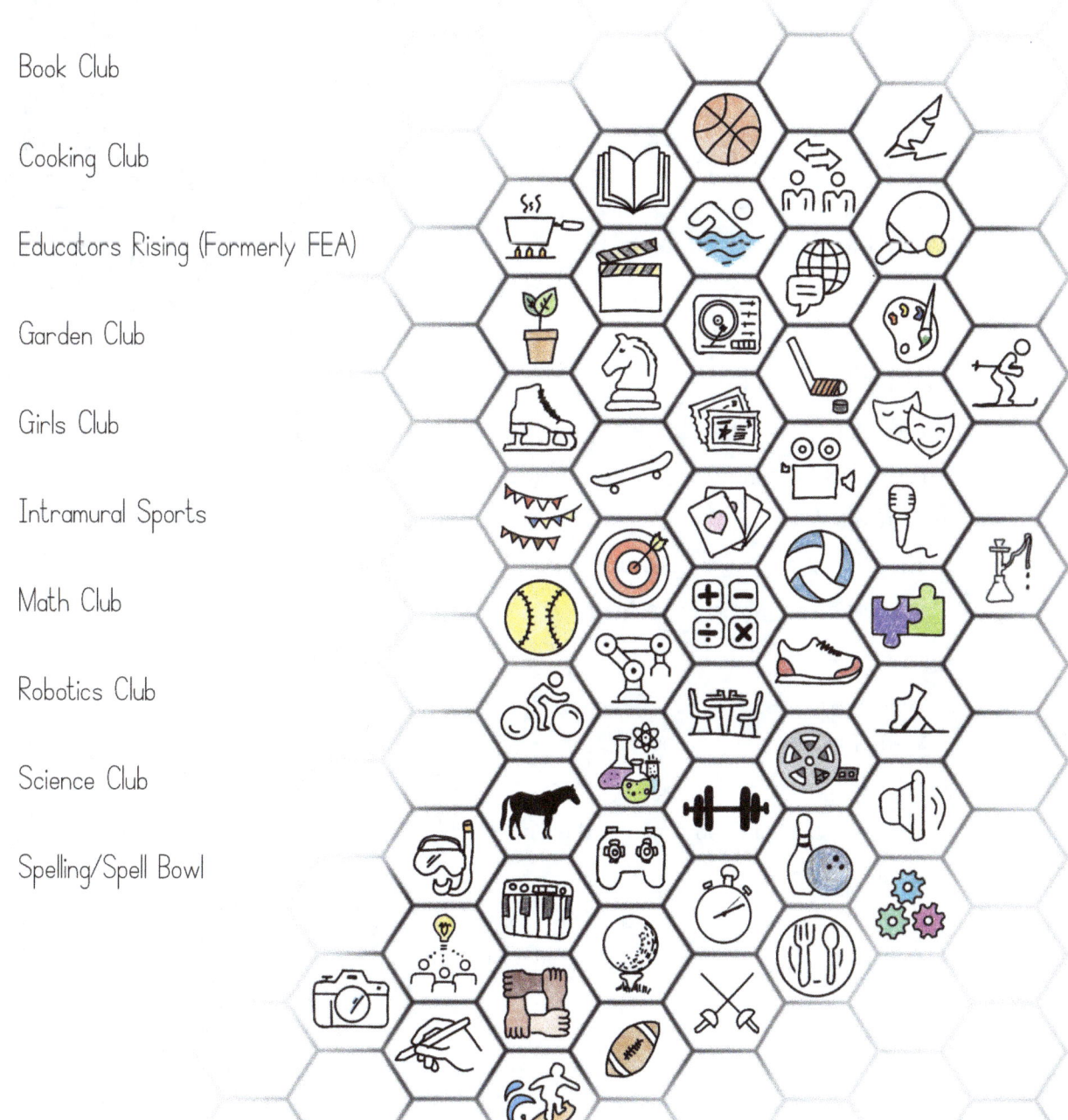

Recommended Reading List

Fiction

Are You There God? It's Me Margaret by Judy Blume

Because of Winn Dixie by Katie DiCamillo

Bootcamp by Todd Strasser

Bud, Not Buddy by Christopher Paul Curtis

Dear Mr. Henshaw by Beverly Clearly

Holes by Louis Sachar

Just as Long as We're Together by Judy Blume

The Fault in Our Stars by John Greene

The Giver by Lois Lowry

The Lord of the Flies by William Golding

The Outsiders by S. E. Hinton

We Were Here by Matt de la Pena

Non Fiction

Be the One: Six True Stories of Teens Overcoming Hardship with Hope by Byron Pitts

Brown Girl Dreaming by Jacqueline Woodson

Girl Rising: Changing the World One Girl at a Time by Tanya Lee Stone

Grace, Gold, Glory: My Leap of Faith by Gabby Douglass

I Am Malala by Malala Yousafzi

Ignite Your Spark: Discovering Who You Are from the Inside Out by Patricia Wooster

I Got This by Laurie Hernandez

Maniac Magee by Jerry Spinelli

Portraits of Jewish-American Heroes by Malta Drucker and Elizabeth Rosen

Shackles from the Deep: Tracing the Path of a Slave Ship, A Bitter Past, and a Rich Legacy by Michael Cotton

The Best We Could Do: An Illustrated Memoir by Thi Bui

The Diary of a Young Girl Anne by Anne Frank

Fantasy

Beautiful Creatures by Kami Garcia and Margaret Stohl

Divergent by Veronica Roth

Harry Potter and The Sorcerer's Stone by J. K. Rowling

I Am Number Four by Pittacus Lore

Island of the Blue Dolphins by Scott O'Dell

Maximum Ride by James Patterson

Percy Jackson and the Lightening Thief by Rick Riordan

The Chronicles of Narnia by C. S. Lewis

The Giver by Lois Lowry

The Hobbit by J. R. R. Tolkien

The Hunger Games by Suzanne Collins

The Maze Runner by James Dashner

Wishtree by Katherine Applegate

Parent Resources

The following are online resources to support your child's academic development and to enhance skills outside of school.

www.abcya.com (some content is free; subscription plans and pricing vary)

www.commonsense.org/education/website/facing-history-and-ourselves (Social Justice- free!)

www.flocavocabulary.com (subscription -plans and pricing vary)

www.funbrain.com (English and Math-free!)

www.icivics.com (Social Studies-free!)

www.ixl.com (English, Math, Science, Social Studies-subscription required)

www.mobymax.com (English and Math-subscription-plans and pricing vary)

www.mrnussbaum.com (Academic games-free!)

www.kahnacademy.org (Math tutorials-free!)

www.softschools.com (Language Arts games-free!)

The following information is to help you deal with the changing attitudes and moods of your middle schooler.

Surviving Your Middle Schooler's Changing Behavior

https://www.scholastic.com/parents/family-life/social-emotional-learning/development- milestones/survive-your-middle-schoolers-changing-behavior.html

Middle School Changes

https://theparentcue.org/middle-school-changes/

The Changes of Middle School

https://www.psychologytoday.com/us/blog/surviving-your-childs-adolescence/201701/social-challenges-middle-school

Developmental Milestones for Typical Middle-Schoolers

https://www.understood.org/en/learning-attention-issues/signs-symptoms/developmental-milestones/developmental-milestones-for-typical-middle-schoolers

Middle School Issues Commonly Faced by Kids

https://www.verywellfamily.com/common-middle-school-problems-kids-encounter-3288140

If there is a book you want to read, but it hasn't been written yet, then you must write it.
— Toni Morrison —

Melody A. Howard holds a B.A. in English from Indiana University, an M.A. in English from Butler University, and an M.S. in Adult Education from Indiana University. She spent over a decade as a college professor, teaching courses such as African American Literature, College Life and Success Skills, Composition, First-Year Experience, and Romantic Love.

In 2014, she transitioned to public school education in Kentucky, where she taught 8th grade Language Arts and helped prepare students for high school. In 2018, she returned to her childhood middle school to teach 6th grade Language Arts. The inspiration for *The Middle School Manual* came to her during this time and, as she describes it, was "inspired by God, and her daughter." Her daughter inspired her to stop working on her memoir and shift her focus to the needs of students and write a practical guide to help them succeed. As a mother and educator, she understands the transition from elementary school to middle school is even more daunting today than any other time in history, thanks to social media and various other social ideologies students must navigate.

In addition to teaching, Ms. Howard coached track at Northview Middle School, and now she enjoys running half marathons throughout Indiana. She hopes The Middle School Manual will inspire and motivate students to succeed academically, personally, and socially. It is her heartfelt prayer that this book helps students achieve their goals—and even more than they ever imagined possible.